PROJECT BOOK

Two per borrower please

'1

2

Clothes in VICTORIAN TIMES

Gill Munton

based on an original text by
Lyn Gash

WAYLAND

Victorian Times

Christmas in Victorian Times

Clothes in Victorian Times

Schools in Victorian Times

Streets in Victorian Times

Sundays in Victorian Times

Transport in Victorian Times

How we learn about the Victorians

Queen Victoria reigned from 1837 to 1901, a time when Britain went through enormous social and industrial changes. We can learn about Victorians in various ways. We can still see many of their buildings standing today, we can look at their documents, maps and artefacts – many of which can be found in museums. Photography, invented during Victoria's reign, gives us a good picture of life in Victorian Britain. In this book you will see what Victorian life was like through some of this historical evidence.

Editor: Carron Brown
Designer: Joyce Chester
Consultant: Norah Granger

First published in 1998 by Wayland Publishers Ltd, 61 Western Road, Hove, East Sussex BN3 1JD, England.

© Copyright 1998 Wayland Publishers Ltd

Find Wayland on the Internet at http://www.wayland.co.uk

British Library Cataloguing in Publication Data
Munton, Gill
    Clothes in Victorian Times. – (Victorian times)
    1.Clothing and dress – History – 19th century – Juvenile literature 2.Costume – Great Britain – History – 19th century – Juvenile literature
    I.Title
    391'.00941
ISBN 0 7502 1880 0

Typeset in England by Joyce Chester
Printed and bound in Italy by G. Canale C.S.p.A., Turin

Text based on *Victorian Life: Clothes* by Lyn Gash published in 1993 by Wayland Publishers Ltd.

Cover picture: This picture shows a woman choosing a new dress to wear.

Picture acknowledgements
Barnardos 15; Birmingham Central Library 27; Bridgeman Art Library *cover*, 4; The Butterick Archives, New York 25 (bottom); Cambridge University Library 19 (bottom); Mary Evans 9, 10, 20, 21 (top), 23, 24; Hulton Deutsch Collection 6 (top), 8, 12, 13 (top), 17 (bottom), 25 (top), 26; Illustrated London News 7; Museum of Costume and Fashion Research, Bath 13 (bottom), 14; Norfolk Museums Service (Stranger's Hall Museum) 21 (bottom); Popperfoto 6 (bottom), 16; Poppyland Publishing 19 (top); Punch Picture Library 22; Regimental Museum, Norwich 17 (top); Victoria & Albert Museum 5, 18.

Contents

Clothes for Women

Rich Victorians liked to wear fashionable new clothes. This was to show other people how important they were. They wore different clothes for different times of the day such as morning, afternoon and evening.

Following the Fashion

Everyone tried to copy the clothes that rich people wore. There were pictures of these clothes in magazines, and people could look at the material in shops. This picture shows a man and a woman who have just got married. They are wearing very smart clothes. Look at the poor family behind the coach. Their clothes are very different.

This rich couple have just got married. ▶

Clothes in Early Victorian Times

Many women wore dresses made from tartan material. Queen Victoria even made up her own tartan pattern. This photograph was taken in the 1840s. It shows Mrs Maria Jane Wood wearing a tartan dress with a long, full skirt. Look at the sleeves. It must have been difficult for Mrs Wood to move her arms.

◀ This woman is wearing an early Victorian dress.

Clothes in Late Victorian Times

Women wore very full skirts in the 1850s and 1860s. In the 1870s, all the fullness was in the back of the skirt. This photograph was taken in 1878. The long piece of material at the back of the woman's dress was called a train. Trains were often decorated with lace and frills.

These people are wearing late Victorian clothes. ▶

Mourning Clothes

If someone in the family died, the relatives all wore dark clothes for a few weeks. These were called mourning clothes. They showed that the wearers were feeling sad. This photograph shows Queen Victoria in mourning for her husband, Prince Albert. He died from an illness called typhoid in 1861. Queen Victoria wore dark clothes such as these for the rest of her life.

◀ This photograph of Queen Victoria was taken in 1875.

Sports Clothes for Women

In early Victorian times, most women did not take part in sport. If they wanted to run, their long skirts got in the way. If they wanted to ride a horse, they had to sit sideways on the saddle. After 1880, women began to play tennis and golf, and to ride bicycles. They wore shorter skirts and looser sleeves, but their clothes were still not very comfortable.

These women are cycling in Hyde Park in London. ▶

Beach Clothes

Suntans were not fashionable in Victorian times. People kept all their clothes on when they sat on the beach, and women carried parasols to keep the sun off their faces. In the 1870s, women began swimming in the sea. They wore thick swimming costumes that covered their bodies and legs. They had to put their costumes on in special huts. There were swimming costumes for men as well.

This is a drawing of the beach at St Leonard's-on-Sea in 1892. ▼

Clothes for Men

During the Victorian period, men began wearing more comfortable clothes, such as those worn for hunting, during the day. Most men preferred these to their other clothes, which were dark and heavy.

Following the Fashion

Rich men could afford to buy expensive material and pay tailors to make their clothes. They also had servants to keep their clothes clean. The man on the right of this picture is wearing a dressing gown over his clothes, because he is relaxing at home. His two visitors have taken their hats off. Men always did this before they went into a house. When they went out, men usually wore hats. They raised their hats or touched them when they met someone they knew on the street.

This picture shows a family at home in 1877. ▼

Clothes in Early Victorian Times

These four men are very fashionably dressed.

They are wearing:

- big bow ties
- frock coats
- watch chains
- fancy waistcoats
- patterned trousers

Their hair-styles and moustaches are fashionable too.

▲ This cartoon was printed in the magazine *Punch* in 1850. The cartoon is making fun of their big bow ties.

Clothes in Late Victorian Times

Look at the photograph on the right. As you can see, men's clothes became much plainer in late Victorian times. Jackets were shorter, and men often wore them with matching trousers and waistcoats. Trousers did not have creases or turn-ups. These did not become popular until the 1890s.

The photograph of the men above was taken in the 1870s. ▲

◄ This photograph shows a wedding in the 1890s.

Wedding Clothes

Most Victorian bridegrooms wore top hats, frock coats and white ties. Can you see the bridegroom in the photograph on page 10? His starched collar, cuffs and shirt-front are fixed to his shirt with studs.

Brides wore ordinary dresses which they could wear again after the wedding. White wedding dresses were not popular until the 1880s.

Sports Clothes

Rich Victorian men had a different outfit for each sport. They often wore these clothes at home as well. The Prince of Wales wore a Homburg hat when he went hunting, and this became a popular style of hat for Victorian men.

Poorer people had to do sports in their ordinary clothes. The woman in this picture has tied up her skirt to keep it clean.

These people are shooting partridges in Norfolk, in 1888. ▲

Clothes for Children

Poor children had to go to work when they were 11 years old or even younger. Their clothes had to be hard-wearing. Rich children had to be quiet and still most of the time. They wore uncomfortable clothes that were smaller versions of the clothes adults wore.

Clothes for Young Children

The child in this picture is a boy. Boys wore dresses until they were about 5 years old, and sometimes they had long hair. This was called 'being in petticoats'.

◀ This photograph was taken in 1857.

Clothes for Girls

Girls' dresses were like the ones their mothers wore, but with shorter skirts. They even wore tight corsets as their mothers did. When they were about 15 years old, they began wearing long skirts and tying their hair up.

◄ This photograph of a girl and her mother was taken in 1876.

▼ The boy below is wearing a sailor suit.

Clothes for Boys

Boys wore breeches or short trousers with tunics. When they were about 10 years old they wore clothes like the ones their fathers wore. Poor boys' clothes were often given to them by their fathers or older brothers. The sleeves and trousers were usually shortened.

This boy is wearing a sailor suit. Sailor suits were cheap and comfortable, and they became very popular.

School Clothes

This photograph shows what many Victorian children wore at school. Many of the children are wearing fashionable clothes although they are quite poor. Most of the girls are wearing pinafores to keep their dresses clean. Boots were very expensive. You can see from the soles of their shoes that they were mended many times before a child could have new ones.

Clothes for Poor Children

Very poor children had to wear second-hand clothes. Many parents could not afford shoes for their children, and so the children could not go to school in bad weather. This photograph shows a group of poor boys in 1870. Most of the boys are wearing hats although they have no shoes.

Clothes for Workers

Some workers, such as railwaymen, postmen and policemen, had to wear uniforms. Fishermen and farm workers needed comfortable, hard-wearing clothes.

Clothes for Servants

Women servants wore dark clothes for doing dirty jobs, and a black dress with a white apron for opening the door to visitors in the afternoon.

Very rich families had menservants who wore brightly coloured uniforms called livery. Most menservants wore much plainer clothes.

This photograph shows a housekeeper and servants in 1886. ▶

Clothes for Soldiers

This photograph shows soldiers of the First Battalion in 1870. ▼

Each regiment of soldiers had its own style of uniform. Officers' uniforms were the most expensive. Soldiers wore their full uniform for parades and in battle. If they were training or doing jobs they could wear simpler clothes.

After the Crimean War (1853–56), uniforms became more comfortable. They were made of khaki material as the old-fashioned red jackets were easy targets in battle.

Clothes for Policemen

The first policemen wore blue frock coats, blue or white trousers and stiff top hats. They had letters and numbers on their collars to show that they were policemen.

In 1864, the uniform became more strict, and policemen had to wear helmets and tunics.

The first truncheons were used in 1856, and the first police whistles were used in 1884.

This is Tom Smith, who was a London policeman in the 1850s and 1860s. ▲

Clothes for Workmen

Most workmen wore:

- jackets
- trousers
- waistcoats
- shirts without collars
- strong boots or clogs
- scarves

Their clothes were made of corduroy or moleskin. By 1890, workmen had started to wear caps.

▲ These porters had to carry heavy loads on their heads. The leather pads helped them to do this.

Clothes for Farm Workers and Fishermen

Farm workers wore old-fashioned breeches and smocks. Fishermen wore waterproof trousers and tunics over knitted jumpers such as the ones in the photograph at the top of page 19. Different patterns of stitching were used in different parts of Britain. Fishermen also wore legwarmers and thick socks.

▲ These fishermen lived in Norfolk.

Clothes for Working Women

Many women worked in coal mines, brickworks and fishing ports. They wore padded trousers because these were easier to work in than skirts. Some Victorians were shocked at the idea of women wearing men's clothes.

This is Ellen Grounds, who was working in a coal mine in 1873. She is wearing an apron over her trousers. ▶

Underwear

Some Victorian underwear was made of red flannel. People thought that this material kept illness away. Women wore corsets, and steel or whalebone frames under their dresses. Victorian underwear was not very comfortable.

Corsets

All women and girls wore corsets to make their waists look small. Corsets were very tight, and women often fainted because they could not breathe properly. This woman is wearing a starched corset which has pieces of steel or whalebone sewn into it. Corsets had to be laced up at the back.

◀ The woman in this picture, drawn in 1897, is wearing a corset.

Crinolines

Crinolines were very wide frames which women wore under their dresses in the 1850s and 1860s. Women often knocked things over with their wide skirts, or set objects on fire by knocking over a candle or an oil lamp by mistake. Wind could blow a skirt up in the air, so women wore long pants to cover their legs.

This woman is putting on her crinoline. ▼

Bustles

After crinolines, bustles became fashionable. Bustles were small frames which held up the material to the backs of the dresses.

By 1890, most women were wearing close-fitting dresses instead of crinolines or bustles.

This kind of bustle was worked by a spring. ▶ It folded up when the woman sat down.

Underwear for Men

Early Victorian men wore cotton shirts and leggings under their clothes. In the 1870s, woollen combinations became popular. People thought wool was healthier than cotton.

This is a cartoon from the magazine *Punch* in 1876. It shows combinations drying in the wind! ▼

"O WILD WEST WIND!"

WALKING ABROAD IN ONE OF HIS LOFTIEST MOODS, AND SEEKING FOR INSPIRATION ON A LONELY HEATH, OUR YOUTHFUL POET COMES UPON A LAUNDRY-YARD, AND SEES UNDER-GARMENTS OF ALL SIZES FLAUNTING IN THE GALE.
[*Lest the susceptibilities of the more refined should be shocked, we hasten to state that the habiliments depicted above belong exclusively to the Male Sex.*

Keeping Clothes Clean

The Victorians did not have washing machines or dryers, so washing clothes was hard work. They did have irons, but these were heavy and difficult to use.

Rich people had plenty of clothes, so the same clothes did not have to be washed every week. Poor people had a wash day every week. Rich people had servants do the washing for them.

▲ These women are washing clothes by hand, and hanging them up to dry.

Buying Clothes

Most clothes were made by dressmakers or tailors. People who lived in towns could buy material from shops, but people who lived in the country had to wait for a pedlar to call.

Salons

Salons were places where dress designers sold their clothes to very rich women. Models walked up and down the room wearing the latest styles, and the customers decided which dresses to have made for them. The customers were then measured by shop assistants, and dressmakers made the dresses for them.

This is a salon in the 1890s. ▶

Dressmakers

Most dressmakers worked at home. The customers gave the dressmakers the material they had chosen, and told them what kind of dress they wanted.

The dressmaker in this picture is using a sewing machine. Sewing machines were invented in 1851.

▲ This dressmaker is working at home.

Paper Patterns

Dressmakers used paper patterns. They pinned the paper shapes on to the material and cut round them to make the different pieces for the dress. The pieces were then sewn together. In the 1840s, women could find paper patterns in magazines. This made it easier for them to make their own clothes. In 1873, the Butterick Company opened a shop selling paper patterns in London.

◄ All these dresses could be made from Butterick patterns.

Department Stores

People could buy hats, shoes and gloves from department stores. These shops also sold some ready-made clothes, which started to become popular, or people could have clothes made up by the stores' dressmakers.

◄ This is Whiteley's department store in London.

The woman on the left is looking at the clothes in a second-hand shop. ▼

Second-hand Clothes Shops

Victorians never threw old clothes away. Rich people gave their old clothes to their servants, and poorer people often sold theirs to second-hand shops. Very poor people bought all their clothes from these shops.

Hand-me-downs

In many families, only the eldest child had new clothes. When he or she grew out of them, the clothes were given to the younger children. These clothes were called hand-me-downs.

▲ The boy on the left is wearing a dress. It was probably handed down by an elder sister.

Timeline

Early 1800s

1829
The first police force is set up in London.

1836
Dressmakers begin using elastic in clothes.

1837
Victoria becomes queen.

1840s

1846
The young Prince of Wales is often seen wearing a sailor suit. This becomes a popular fashion for boys.

1849
Safety pins are invented.

1850s

Crinolines become popular.

1851
Tartan becomes fashionable.

1851
Sewing machines are invented.

1860s

1861
Prince Albert dies.

1864
Policemen begin wearing tunics and helmets.

1870s

Bustles become popular.

1873
The Butterick Company opens a shop selling paper patterns in London.

1880s

Soldiers begin wearing khaki uniforms.

1886
A book called *Little Lord Fauntleroy* is published. Velvet suits become fashionable for boys, because Little Lord Fauntleroy wore them.

1890s

People begin to use coat hangers.

Soldiers in the Boer War wear khaki uniforms in battle.

1900s

1901
Queen Victoria dies.

Glossary

Breeches Short trousers that fasten just below the knees.

Bustles Frames that held up dresses at the back.

Combinations Underwear in one piece – vest and pants joined together.

Corsets Tight, stiff undergarments. Women wore corsets to make their waists look small.

Crinolines Wide frames that held women's skirts out from their bodies.

Flannel Woollen material that was used for making underwear.

Frills Decorative material that is gathered together, usually used to make wavy edging to clothes.

Frock coats Long coats wore by Victorian men.

Homburg hat A hat made of felt. It has a dent in the top and a turned-up brim.

Khaki A dust-coloured cloth which is used for making soldiers' uniforms.

Lace Decorative material made from thread and holes put together in pretty patterns.

Moleskin A hard-wearing cotton cloth which was used for making work clothes.

Parasols Sunshades shaped like umbrellas.

Pedlar A kind of travelling salesman.

Smocks Loose shirts worn by farm workers.

Studs Buttons on the front of a shirt used to connect the cuffs and shirt-front to the shirt.

Tailors People who work by making men's jackets and trousers.

Tunics Loose shirts worn with belts.

Books to Read

Chamberlain, E. R., *Everyday Life in Victorian Times* (Simon & Schuster Young Books, 1993)

Morley, *Clothes* (Timelines series, Watts, 1992)

Tames, Richard, *What Do We Know About the Victorians?* (Simon & Schuster Young Books, 1994)

Thomson, Ruth, *Clothes* (Changing Times series, Watts, 1992)

Ventura, Piero, *Clothes Through the Ages* (Simon & Schuster Young Books, 1993)

Places to Visit

England

Avon: The Museum of Costume, The Assembly Rooms, Bennet Street, Bath, BA1 2QH. Tel: 01225 477789

Birmingham: City Museum and Art Gallery, Chamberlain Square, Birmingham, B3 3DH. Tel: 0121 2352834

Devon: The Devonshire Collection of Costume, Bogan House, High Street, Totnes, TQ9 5RY. Tel: 01803 862423 Paulise de Bush Collection, National Trust Collection of Costume, Killerton House, Broadclyst, Exeter, EX5 3LE. Tel: 01392 881691 Rougement House, Museum of Costume and Lace, Castle Street, Exeter, EX4 3PU. Tel: 01392 265858

Leicester: Wygston's House, Museum of Costume, Applegate, Leicester. Tel: 01533 554100

London: The Victoria & Albert Museum, South Kensington, London, SW7 2RL. Tel: 0171 9388500

Manchester: The Gallery of English Costume, Platt Hall, Rusholme, M14 5LL. Tel: 0161 2245217

Norfolk: Strangers' Hall Museum, 4 Charing Cross, Norwich, NR2 4AL. Tel: 01603 667229

Nottinghamshire: Museum of Costumes and Textiles, Castle Gate, Nottingham, NG1 6AF. Tel: 0115 9483504

Yorkshire: Castle Howard Costume Galleries, Castle Howard, Malton, York, YO6 7DA. Tel: 01653 84333

Northern Ireland

Ulster: Ulster Museum, Botanic Gardens, Belfast, BT9 5AB. Tel: 01232 381251

Scotland

Dumfries and Galloway: Shambellie House, Museum of Costume, New Abbey, Dumfries, DG2 8HG. Tel: 01387 85375

Strathclyde: Paisley Museum and Art Gallery, High Street, Paisley, PA1 2BA. Tel: 0141 8893151

Wales

Glamorgan: Welsh Folk Museum, St Fagan's Castle, Cardiff, CF5 6XB. Tel: 01222 569441

Index